ALSO AVAILABLE IN THIS SERIES:
BELIEVE: The Words and Inspiration of Desmond Tutu
PEACE: The Words and Inspiration of Mahatma Gandhi
LOVE: The Words and Inspiration of Mother Teresa

Produced and originated by PQ Blackwell Limited
116 Symonds Street, Auckland, New Zealand
www.pqblackwell.com

Distributed exclusively in the United States, Canada, and the Philippines by Blue Mountain Arts, Inc.

Designed by Cameron Gibb, Annatjie Matthee, and Carolyn Lewis.

Printed by Midas Printing International Ltd., China.

Library of Congress Control Number: 2006909704
ISBN: 978-1-59842-240-5

Acknowledgments appear on page 94.

First Printing: 2007

Blue Mountain Arts, Inc.
P.O. Box 4549, Boulder, Colorado 80306

THE WORDS AND INSPIRATION OF

MARTIN LUTHER KING, JR.

INTRODUCTION BY
ARCHBISHOP DESMOND TUTU

Blue Mountain Press ®
Boulder, Colorado

"If I diminish you, I diminish myself."

In my culture and tradition the highest praise that can be given to someone is, *"Yu, u nobuntu,"* an acknowledgment that he or she has this wonderful quality, *ubuntu.* It is a reference to their actions toward their fellow human beings, it has to do with how they regard people and how they see themselves within their intimate relationships, their familial relationships, and within the broader community. *Ubuntu* addresses a central tenet of African philosophy: the essence of what it is to be human.

The definition of this concept has two parts. The first is that the person is friendly, hospitable, generous, gentle, caring, and compassionate. In other words, someone who will use their strengths on behalf of others — the weak and the poor and the ill — and not take advantage of anyone. This person treats others as he or she would be treated. And because of this they express the second part of the concept, which concerns openness, large-heartedness. They share their worth. In doing so my humanity is recognized and becomes inextricably bound to theirs.

People with *ubuntu* are approachable and welcoming; their attitude is kindly and well-disposed; they are not threatened by the goodness in others because their own esteem and self-worth is generated by knowing they belong to a greater whole. To recast the Cartesian proposition "I think, therefore I am," *ubuntu* would phrase it, "I am human because I belong." Put another way, "a person is a person through other people," a concept perfectly captured by the phrase "me we." No one comes into the world fully formed. We would not know how to think or walk or speak or behave unless we learned it from our fellow human beings. We need other human beings in order to be human. The solitary, isolated human being is a contradiction in terms.

Because we need one another, our natural tendency is to be cooperative and helpful. If this were not true we would have died out as a species long ago, consumed by our violence and hate. But we haven't. We have kept on despite the evil and the wars that have brought so much suffering and misery down the centuries. We have kept on because we strive for harmony and community, a community not only of the living but also one that honors our forebears. This link to the past gives us a sense of continuity, a sense that we have created and create societies that are meant to be for the greater good and try to overcome anything that subverts our purpose. Our wars end; we seek to heal.

But anger, resentment, a lust for revenge, greed, even the aggressive competitiveness that rules so much of our contemporary world, corrodes and jeopardizes our harmony. *Ubuntu* points out that those who seek to destroy and dehumanize are also victims — victims, usually, of a pervading ethos, be it a political ideology, an economic system, or a distorted religious conviction. Consequently, they are as much dehumanized as those on whom they trample.

Never was this more obvious than during the apartheid years in South Africa. All humanity is interlinked. Thus, the humanity of the perpetrators of apartheid was inexorably bound to that of their victims. When they dehumanized another by inflicting suffering and harm, they dehumanized themselves. In fact I said at the time that the oppressor was dehumanized as much as, if not more than, those oppressed. How else could you interpret the words of the minister of police, Jimmy Kruger, on hearing of the death of Black Consciousness leader, Steve Biko, in prison. Of his tortured and painful killing, Kruger said, it "leaves me cold." You have to ask what has happened to the humanity — the *ubuntu* — of someone who could speak so callously about the suffering and death of a fellow human being.

It was equally clear that recovering from this situation would require a magnanimousness on the part of the victims if there was to be a future. The end of apartheid, I knew, would put *ubuntu* to the test. Yet I never doubted its power of reconciliation. In fact I often recalled the words of a man called Malusi Mpumlwana, an associate of Biko's, who, even while he was being tortured by the security police, looked at his torturers and realized that these were human beings too and that they needed him "to help them recover the humanity they [were] losing."

The essence of *ubuntu*, or "me we," shines so clearly in the life and actions of Martin Luther King, Jr. King depicts the recognition that our responsibility is not only toward the community of the living but our ancestors as well. He sought to achieve human rights for black Americans and thereby humanize their slave forebears. For him it meant enduring state harassment, imprisonment, and ultimately, assassination. Yet he never wavered in his commitment to others.

His *ubuntu* showed that the only way we can ever be human is together. The only way we can be free is together.

The Most Reverend Desmond M. Tutu, OMSG DD FKC
Anglican Archbishop Emeritus of Cape Town

Martin Luther King, Jr.

1929 – 1968

Surely those who are reluctant to do what is asked of them should be the more admired. Surely those who are afraid, who question themselves, who doubt their own abilities, but who, under pressure, rise to the moment, are our true paragons. Surely the man facing a mass of restless people, who puts aside his prepared speech to say those hauntingly beautiful words — "I have a dream..." — surely this man becomes the zeitgeist.

"I say to you today, my friends: so even though we face the difficulties of today and tomorrow, I still have a dream... I have a dream that one day on the red hills of Georgia the sons of former slaves and the sons of former slave-owners will be able to sit down together at the table of brotherhood. I have a dream that one day even the state of Mississippi will be transformed into an oasis of freedom and justice.

"I have a dream..."[1]

With that speech Martin Luther King, Jr. realized the hopes of two hundred and fifty thousand people gathered at the Lincoln Memorial in Washington, D.C. It was the largest civil rights demonstration ever held in the United States, and after a hot summer's afternoon of political speeches the crowd was listlessly beginning to fray on the edges. But when that soaring, powerful voice began those rhythmic and cadenced sentences, people became rooted, silent. And when he had finished and stood there beaded in sweat and took a step back from the microphones, for a moment, a brief moment, there was a stunned acknowledgment of what King had said. Then a roar of acceptance rose from tens of thousands of throats in tribute to the man who had articulated their lives. Across the country, millions more watched a live television broadcast: the moral force of black America's demands for equality was undeniable.

At the end of that year, 1963, this man, Martin Luther King, Jr., would be proclaimed *Time* magazine's Man of the Year. The following year, he would be awarded the Nobel Peace Prize, at thirty-five, the youngest peace prize-winner ever, and only the third black man to receive the honor. In the eyes of his followers and those whose suffering he portrayed, he had become an icon, but it was not a status King sought. Rather it had been thrust on him and, in a sense, forced him to confront his destiny: the threats, the arrests, the harassment, and, eventually, the assassination. In public he was a man of the people, in private he was a reluctant hero. But he was well aware of his own qualities, and because of this empathized with people, both those he led and those whose fears he challenged.

"We often develop inferiority complexes and we stumble through life with a feeling of insecurity, a lack of self confidence, and a sense of impending failure," he told his congregation one Sunday in 1967, a year before he was killed. "A fear of what life may bring encourages some persons to wander aimlessly along the frittering road of excessive drink and sexual promiscuity. I know this. I know it from my own personal experiences."[2]

This was King in an hour of truthfulness when he needed to reach out to ordinary people in the hopes of arousing their understanding that while he might be the man at the head of the protest marches, the man calling for freedom in the face of police violence, the man incarcerated, he was, too, as vulnerable as were they. And yet, when the hour came, King was quick to put aside his anxieties and face any hardship no matter how frightening. Then, undaunted, he would act on their behalf. In that selfless courage lay his capacity to inspire.

Martin Luther King, Jr. was born on January 15, 1929 in Atlanta, Georgia, the heartland of the American South, a place deeply segregated and riven by entrenched racial attitudes and atrocities toward black people. It was the headquarters of the white racist organization, the violent Ku Klux Klan. But King's family was well off for a southern black family, and although they were subjected to discrimination, they suffered no economic hardship during the American Depression years. In fact, little distinguished their lifestyle from any middle-class family in America. The King's home was comfortable, they dressed well, ate well, and enjoyed the fellowship of a close-knit community, with the church where King, Sr. preached a second home to the young boy. King's childhood was happy and contented, protected by the love of his family and influenced by the imposing presence of his father, who strode through the streets, a community patriarch and a leader in civic affairs.

However, the hurtful realities of racism were only ever a remark away. For King that remark pierced through the protective idyll when he was just six years old. He had befriended a white child whose father ran a grocery store not far from the Kings' house. For several years the boys were close playmates, but when they reached school age and went off to separate schools they saw less of one another, until King was told by the boy's father that the friendship had to end completely. King was shocked, reduced to tears. That night he blurted out the sorry tale to his parents and was gently told some truths about the nature of racism.

If that episode embedded itself in his consciousness, then it was to be inflamed by two further incidents. The first occurred a few years later, when his father took him to buy a pair of shoes. They sat down to wait for assistance only to be told that black people were served in the back of the shop. King, Sr. took his son by the hand and walked out in disgust. A few years later, King was returning by bus from a debating contest when he and his teacher were told to stand so that white passengers could sit. For a long bus trip of several hours the pair had to endure the indignity and fatigue of the socially marginalized. The fourteen-year-old King seethed with anger at the discriminatory injustice of this regulation, realizing that from the moment he had been forbidden to play with his childhood friend he had started hating white people.

"As I grew older and older, this feeling continued to grow [even though] my parents would always tell me that I should not hate the white man, but that it was my duty, as a Christian, to love him."[3]

And yet despite this apparently adamant position, King's opinions changed radically when he entered Moorhouse College in September 1944. Partly this occurred because of the books he read, partly because he mixed with young white people who shared his ideals of racial and economic justice. It was there he discovered Henry David Thoreau's essay "On Civil Disobedience" and learned about the author's theory of nonviolent resistance, which ultimately landed Thoreau in jail. It was at Moorhouse that King, only fifteen years old, began to think of noncooperation as a means of confronting the evil he saw poisoning his society. He joined student bodies working for racial justice and sat on the Intercollegiate Council — a mixed-race body — that softened his attitudes toward white people.

It dawned on him that racial hatreds were driven by attitudes deeply ingrained in society rather than by individual convictions. At the personal level, people were people. Simultaneously, he felt an urge to serve society, and his thoughts turned to a career in medicine or law, although behind these possibilities was always the pull of the ministry. For eighteen months King remained skeptical about religion, wondering if it had the intellectual foundations he sought, especially as he was embarrassed by the foot stamping and shouting of emotionally charged Southern congregations. But after taking a course in the philosophy of religion, the academically astute King saw ways to bind his all-encompassing attitudes toward humanity with the power of the pulpit. With a nod to the influence of his father, he decided to enter the ministry.

But first King undertook a self-imposed rite of passage: he went to work in the railyards and trucking stations of Atlanta. Until then King had led a sheltered life, largely unaware of the conditions under which poor black people lived and worked. If he was to pursue a career in the ministry, how could he do so with authenticity if he did not know how his congregation suffered? He needed to experience the life of an unskilled worker, even though his parents tried to persuade him otherwise.

To begin with, King worked in depots unloading trains and trucks. He talked to his coworkers — both blacks and whites — and learned about their lives, the nights they and their children went hungry to bed, their destitution, the degrading circumstances of their homes. He became, like them, yet another "nigger" in the eyes of the white bosses. He saw that although whites did the same work as blacks, they were less humiliated, bore fewer indignities, and were paid slightly more. Toward the end of summer King went north to seek work in the tobacco fields of Connecticut. This was hard and exhausting labor, but the overseers were more respectful, and because the state was desegregated he could eat in any restaurant, sit anywhere in a cinema. The evil of the racial policies in the South was thrown into sharp relief. When going home by train at the end of summer, he was forced to eat at the rear of the dining car and a curtain was closed to separate him from the white diners. The shame again overwhelmed him. He felt as if the curtain obliterated his sense of self, as if he'd become an invisible man.

That summer of backbreaking manual labor cast a long shadow on the life of Martin Luther King, Jr. It tempered his understanding of people's personal sufferings, deepened his intellectual ideals with the empathy of experience, and most importantly, gave him the courage to act on his convictions no matter at what personal cost.

For the next three years, King was a student at the Crozer Theological Seminary at Chester, Pennsylvania. This was a small college of a hundred students, only half a dozen of whom were black. Again King experienced the freedom of desegregation as the dormitories were mixed. However, his first year was not without its incidents.

Some months into the semester King was confronted by an angry white Southern student who had been the victim of a dormitory joke. The student, believing King the instigator, barged into King's room waving a pistol and had to be subdued by other students. Throughout the incident King remained calm, if frightened. When peace was restored, he brushed off the incident and declined to press charges. Not long after this King and four friends were in a restaurant in nearby New Jersey. The white owner refused to serve them and the four refused to leave until he did. Outraged, the man drew a gun and threatened them before running outside and discharging a round into the air. Again King's reaction was quiet and placatory. He and his friends left, returning later with a policeman. They pressed charges, but when a group of white student witnesses withdrew their supportive statements, the matter was dropped.

 These incidents aside, King immersed himself in his studies at Crozer, laying the intellectual foundation that was to support him through the demanding years ahead. A dedicated student, he spent most of his time on his work, gradually improving his marks until in his final year he scored straight As. He also enrolled at the University of Pennsylvania to take a course in philosophy, and it was there that he came across the work of the German philosopher Hegel and the American theologian Walter Rauschenbusch. Hegel's argument that leaders were the instruments of public will particularly intrigued King, but it was Rauschenbusch's assertion that the church should take an active and leading role in the struggle for social justice which resonated with his own thinking. He was particularly drawn to Rauschenbusch's optimism — which reinforced his own sanguine disposition — and believed that the power of Christian love would advance his cause. However, he also encountered the more pessimistic views of Reinhold Niebuhr, that human motives were complex and multilayered and that good and evil were not simple concepts. King began to realize that he could not rely on the compassion of Christianity to eradicate the injustice of racism and

discrimination from society. It would take, he acknowledged, more than words to achieve these ends. And then King was introduced to the thoughts and actions of Mohandas Gandhi. The combination of Gandhi's nonviolent *satyagraha* movement with the strikes, boycotts, and mass marches that the Mahatma had initiated during the final decades of British colonial rule in India appealed to King, who felt the circumstances in the United States demanded an active resistance, although the means of resistance should be passive.

King was still a long way from imagining himself at the head of a phalanx of protesters, let alone organizing and maintaining a boycott. His temperament was analytical, and with his academic record, his professors suggested he register for a doctorate in theology. This prospect appealed to him: the quiet life of thought and sermon. King was no rebel. In fact he liked good clothes, felt at ease in fine hotels and restaurants, had made airplane trips and long-distance telephone calls — he even had a bank account. In the presence of whites he was serious, courteous, and personable, as if in deliberate contradiction of the white stereotype of blacks as drunk, loud, and dirty. For all this, and for all his progressive political ideals, his attitude toward women was of its time. When he met Coretta Scott — the woman who would become his wife — he commented to her that she had all the qualities he expected to find in a girl he'd like to have for a wife. The bluntness took Coretta by surprise, but she did put aside her singing career to marry him.

His doctorate complete, King decided to forgo an academic career in favor of the ministry. He told his wife that he liked people too much and had a strong feeling for the masses. He wanted to return to the South to a black parish. Offers from churches both in the North and the South were laid on his desk, but the need to serve his people led him to accept a pastorship at the Dexter Avenue Baptist Church in Montgomery, Alabama. For the next fifteen months the couple enjoyed a happy, untrammelled existence. King finished his thesis, joined various civic committees, and threw himself enthusiastically into his pastoral duties. Coretta was pregnant with their first child, they were surrounded by friends, and life exuded possibilities — never more so than when the baby was born in November 1955. Three weeks later, one of King's parishioners, Rosa Parks, was arrested for refusing to give up her seat on a city bus to a white passenger.

Under the instigation of a civil rights lawyer, the black community decided to boycott the buses. King was part of this initial decision, but it was only a few days later that he accepted a request to act as spokesman for the protest, although he worried about his ability to wear the mantel. It was a courageous decision nevertheless, because as the public face of the hastily formed body fronting the boycott, he would be the target for white anger and retaliation. And in the tinderbox South where clandestine Ku Klux Klan hangings of black activists were still a reality, that retaliation was likely to be violent and deadly.

King's first test was a speech to five thousand supporters. He was nervous, wanting to inspire resistance, but not hate and violence. He stood before the crowd and delivered a rousing call in the tones and with the forcefulness that would become his hallmark.

"We are here this evening for serious business. We are here in a general sense because first and foremost we are American citizens and we are determined to apply our citizenship to the fullness of its meaning. We are here also because of our love for democracy, because of our deep-seated belief that democracy transformed from thin paper to thick action is the greatest form of government on earth…"[4]

That moment determined the rest of King's life: he would be in constant demand, he would be in the public eye, he would be adored and vilified. As he fought the cause of the discriminated, he would lose interest in his dress and appearance and dispense with nonessential possessions. When he won the Nobel Peace Prize, he would donate the $54,000 to the civil rights movement and keep nothing for himself. He would live in rented houses and spartan conditions. The personal cost of his crusade to give ordinary people their dignity would amount to self-sacrifice.

The Montgomery bus boycott lasted a year, ending with a Supreme Court ruling that Alabama's state and local segregation laws were unconstitutional. The day after the court order became effective, King woke early so that he could be the first black passenger on a bus. Throughout the day he rode different buses to ensure there was no trouble.

The Martin Luther King, Jr. who took his place on those buses in December 1956 was in many respects a changed man from the one who had motivated his supporters to transform "thin paper into thick action."

The moment he became the public face of the boycott he became a target. He received threatening late-night phone calls which disturbed him to such a degree that he wondered if he shouldn't step down. He became fearful. Then he was arrested for a minor traffic offense that was nothing short of police harassment. It meant being fingerprinted and locked in a cell with hardened criminals. Although he was bailed out within a few hours, the experience unnerved him. The following evening, having been awoken by yet another ominous phone call and unable to sleep, King sat at his kitchen table, a cup of coffee untouched and growing cold before him. He was ready to give up. He thought about the previous comforts of his life, his cherished baby daughter, and his loyal and devoted wife, and he believed he was losing his courage. And then he heard an inner voice, a voice he took to be that of Jesus, saying, "Martin Luther, stand up for justice. Stand up for truth. And lo I shall be with you. Even until the end of the world."[5] That experience restored King's inner strength. His fears dissipated, his uncertainty waned. He switched off the kitchen light and went upstairs to bed and sleep came instantly. For King that moment was seminal — an epiphany — a time that he would repeatedly recall whenever the doubts came.

Three nights later his house was firebombed. King was at a meeting, but Coretta was in the living room and their daughter was asleep upstairs when the bomb exploded on the porch. His wife and daughter were unharmed and the fire was quickly extinguished. But news of the bombing spread rapidly and an angry mob soon gathered. By the time King arrived, police on the scene began to fear a riot and the tension was at a breaking point. King stepped onto the porch to pacify his supporters:

"I did not start this boycott. I was asked by you to serve as your spokesman, I want it known the length and breadth of this land that if I am stopped this movement will not stop. If I am stopped our work will not stop. For what we are doing is right. What we are doing is just."[6] He told the mob to put away their weapons, that he was not advocating violence no matter how provocative the circumstances. They were to love their enemies.

Before the boycott ended, King, while waiting for his lawyer in a corridor of the Montgomery court, was arrested on a spurious charge of loitering, and at the subsequent court hearing found guilty and sentenced to a fine of ten dollars or fourteen days' imprisonment. It wasn't the first time King had been sentenced to a jail term, but the earlier case had gone to appeal and would eventually be thrown out. Now he was facing jail as a reality. The moment the hearing ended King either had to pay the fine or be handcuffed and led away to the cells. He told the court that he couldn't pay the fine in good conscience because he was deeply concerned about the injustices and indignities his people suffered in a land that cherished the concepts of liberty and equality. He would therefore serve the prison sentence. The outward declaration was brave and firm, but King made it with trepidation. The thought of jail was repellent and frightening. Even fourteen days daunted him. But he knew he had to break his own fear and that of black people, and that the only alternative was to submit himself to that menacing state institution, the Southern jail. "The time has come," he said, "when perhaps only the willing and nonviolent acts of suffering can arouse this nation to wipe out the scourge of brutality and violence inflicted on Negroes."[7] As it happened King didn't have to serve his sentence. The fine was paid by the police chief, fearing public outrage. But King had won a major victory, and when in subsequent boycotts and peaceful demonstrations he called upon people to flood the jails, they heeded his call.

The success of the Montgomery bus boycott convinced black leaders that they needed a coordinating body. Consequently in February 1957 they formed the Southern Christian Leadership Conference (SCLC) with King as president. If the bus boycott had given King a degree of notoriety, he was now propelled onto a city-to-city talk circuit that had him deliver more than two hundred speeches across the country during the year. He became a figure of national prominence.

The following year King's first book, *Stride Toward Freedom*, an account of the bus boycott, appeared and he increased his commitments by embarking on a schedule of public appearances that almost ended tragically. While signing copies at a department store in Harlem, he was stabbed by a black woman who plunged a letter opener into his chest. King was rushed to a hospital, and after a three-hour operation the weapon was removed. The tip had come to rest against a main artery close to his heart. Had he so much as sneezed after the attack, he would have died. His attacker was considered criminally insane and committed to a mental hospital. King held no animosity toward her, concerned only that she got the treatment she needed. The attack, however, brought home to him the high levels of hatred and violence permeating America, be it in the white South or in his own community.

After some months of convalescence, followed by a trip to India to pay tribute to the memory of Gandhi, King returned home convinced that the time was right for more rigorous protests. Reluctantly, and with tearful emotion, he resigned his pastorship, telling his congregation that history had thrust upon him a duty he couldn't ignore. His time was now devoted fully to the SCLC.

For the last seven years of King's short life, he entered a vortex of activity that spun ever faster. His punishing speaking schedule continued, but added to this was a series of civil disobedience actions, arrests, incarcerations, and the ever-present fear of death. The general political climate in the South worsened as the Ku Klux Klan increased its bombings and assassinations. Police brutality in response to the protests only went to ignite already hot tempers.

The first of the clashes occurred in 1960 when students at a campus in Greensboro, North Carolina, started a canteen "sit-in" to protest against segregated lunch counters. The movement quickly spread to other colleges, and the SCLC stepped in to coordinate the action. King, always prepared to lead by example, joined a group of students demonstrating at a department store in Atlanta. The group had agreed that if they were arrested they would go to jail, a decision endorsed by King. Within a few hours the police obliged, and although the students were released with warnings, King was sentenced to a harsh six months' imprisonment and denied bail. Word of King's predicament reached Senator John Kennedy (then involved in presidential elections), and his brother, Robert Kennedy, convinced the judge to grant King bail. Ironically, the Kennedys' intervention may have won JFK the election by swinging the black Southern vote in their favor.

The sit-ins continued and eventually resulted in hundreds of lunch counters desegregating. Encouraged by this success the students embarked on a campaign of "freedom rides" to desegregate transportation facilities across the South. King was asked to chair their committee. He did more than that, joining them in their defiance of segregation laws. The reaction by white extremists was predictably violent: students were hauled from buses and beaten, but the freedom rides continued.

In Albany, Georgia, a racist stronghold, students were arrested, and King led a defiant march to the city hall, protesting the police action. Again everyone was arrested, but in the subsequent negotiations bus and rail stations were desegregated, although the authorities closed parks and libraries rather than integrate them. King organized a massive protest march which had to be called off when the city obtained a court injunction. Dismayed at this reaction but not dispirited, he moved the site of the civil rights struggle to Birmingham, Alabama, a manufacturing city and one of the richest in the South. The two-month campaign was as rough and as risky as King had anticipated. Hundreds were arrested. Again an injunction was granted forbidding marches and demonstrations, but King decided to break it. He dressed in denims and a work shirt — his jail clothes — and led a march on Good Friday, April 12, 1963. Again he was arrested, this time placed in the solitary confinement he dreaded. The reaction of the authorities to the appeal for justice so incensed him that he wrote what was to become a lengthy and impassioned plea for civil disobedience, his "Letter from Birmingham City Jail." A month later, the sheer public pressure of the marches and protests cracked the edifice of racial discrimination in the South.

Over the next four years King was involved in civil rights demonstrations and voter registration campaigns that ranged from Florida in 1963 to Selma, Alabama, in 1965, to Chicago the following year, and on to what became King's last effort, the Poor People's Campaign in 1968. By then the United States had been torn by violent race riots, and King was under severe personal and political pressure. If anything his position had been exacerbated by his condemnation of the war in Vietnam as "but a symptom of a far deeper malady within the American spirit."[8] Many within the civil rights movement thought he was taking a radical stand by commenting on the war, while some of his white supporters considered his opinions unpatriotic. But King remained determined to speak out against injustice wherever he saw it, even though the death threats had never ceased and his safety seemed constantly in jeopardy. When JFK had been assassinated in 1963, King told his wife that a similar fate awaited him; it became a nagging possibility. Yet he kept his anxiety to the deep, dark hours, and only his closest friends knew the fear he had to overcome.

With each demonstration, each march, each sit-in, King realized he was walking a razor's edge. During the Birmingham campaign he felt that at any moment he could be attacked and that it was inevitable that at some point he would be physically hurt. For years he had said that he would not have a long life, but he continued the marches because he had to. "I don't march because I like it," he told one gathering, "I march because I must."[9] Time after time in the final two years of his life he stirred up his followers by talking about the beauty of the marches, the love that had been demonstrated, and the hatred that they had absorbed. Selflessly he travelled from city to city in a punishing schedule to encourage and enthuse his supporters.

On the day before the assassination he spoke at a public meeting in Harlem, recalling the stabbing incident that had almost killed him a decade earlier. He summed up his career by prefacing his major campaigns with the phrase "If I had sneezed" using the rousing cadences that recalled his great "I have a dream" speech. He said, "I don't know what will happen now. We've got some difficult days ahead. But it really doesn't matter with me now because I've been to the mountaintop... I've looked over and seen the promised land. I may not get there with you... [but] I'm not worried about anything. I'm not fearing any man."[10] The emotion of King's speech came from deep within him: he touched on matters that were close to his heart and his personal life, and as always he ended with the rousing optimism that had compelled people to walk behind him in innumerable marches. Those with King that night thought he had revealed himself in a way they had not heard before: he was open, exposed, vulnerable before his followers. Yet the intimacy relaxed him, as if the view from the mountaintop was a profound relief.

The next day King slept late, and in the afternoon joked with his companions, engaging them in a playful pillow fight in his motel room. These sudden expressions of hilarity were not unknown and had the effect of bolstering the spirits of his companions and colleagues. After the rough-and-tumble, the men dispersed to dress for dinner. An hour later King stepped onto the balcony of his first-floor room and paused there debating inwardly whether or not to take a jacket. Somewhere off to his right, a white man named James Earl Ray brought the crosshairs of his rifle sights onto King's neck and fired.

Martin Luther King, Jr., the man who had stood for nonviolence, who wanted equality and justice, died of that gunshot wound an hour later — but the dream did not. Nor did King's words: "I have a dream today. I have a dream that one day every valley shall be exalted, every hill and mountain shall be made low, the rough places will be made plain and the crooked places will be made straight... and all flesh shall see it together."[11]

Mike Nicol
Cape Town, 2006

We must all learn to live together as brothers. Or we will all perish together as fools.

If any of you are around when I have to meet my day, I don't want a long funeral. And if you get somebody to deliver the eulogy, tell them not to talk too long. Every now and then I wonder what I want them to say. Tell them not to mention that I have a Nobel Peace Prize, that isn't important. Tell them not to mention that I have three or four hundred other awards, that's not important. Tell them not to mention where I went to school. I'd like somebody to mention that day, that Martin Luther King, Jr., tried to give his life serving others. I'd like for somebody to say that day, that Martin Luther King, Jr., tried to love somebody. I want you to say that day, that I tried to be right on the war question. I want you to be able to say that day, that I did try to feed the hungry. And I want you to be able to say that day, that I did try, in my life, to clothe those who were naked. I want you to say, on that day, that I did try, in my life, to visit those who were in prison. I want you to say that I tried to love and serve humanity.

{ Extract from the "Drum Major Instinct" sermon, given in February 1968, two months before King's assassination. Excerpts from this sermon were played at his nationally televised funeral service }

1968 }

Forgiveness is not
an occasional act;
it is a permanent
attitude.

I think Alfred Nobel would know what I mean when I say that I accept this award in the spirit of a curator of some precious heirloom which he holds in trust for its true owners — all those to whom beauty is truth and truth beauty — and in whose eyes the beauty of genuine brotherhood and peace is more precious than diamonds or silver or gold.

{ Extract from the Nobel Peace Prize
acceptance speech

1964 }

All humanity is involved in a simple process, and all men are brothers. To the degree that I harm my brother, no matter what he is doing to me, to that extent I am harming myself.

{ Extract from the "Experiment in Love" speech }
1958}

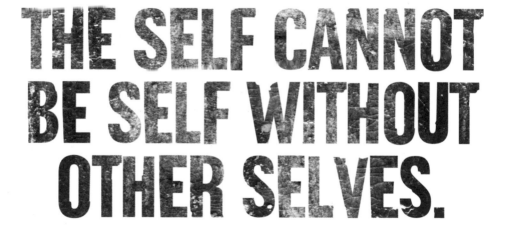

THE SELF CANNOT BE SELF WITHOUT OTHER SELVES.

Hate begets hate; violence begets violence.

The past is strewn with the ruins of
the empires of tyranny, and each is a
monument not merely to man's blunders
but to his capacity to overcome them.

We must meet the forces of hate with
the power of love.

There is within human nature

an amazing potential for goodness.

It may well be that the greatest tragedy of this period of social transition is not the glaring noisiness of the so-called bad people, but the appalling silence of the so-called good people.

The important thing about a man is not the color of his skin or the texture of his hair, but the texture and quality of his soul.

The ultimate measure of a man is not where he stands in moments of comfort and convenience, but where he stands at times of challenge and controversy.

{ "On Being a Good Neighbor" — extract from a sermon delivered at the time of the Montgomery bus protests }

1956}

It is hardly a moral act to encourage others patiently to accept injustice which he himself does not endure.

We are caught in an inescapable network of mutuality, tied in a single garment of destiny. Whatever affects one directly affects all indirectly.

We must come to see that human progress never rolls in on wheels of inevitability… We must use time creatively, and forever realize that the time is always ripe to do right.

{ Extracts from "Letter from Birmingham City Jail" — this public letter was written from jail while King was serving a sentence for participating in civil rights demonstrations in Birmingham, Alabama,

1963 }

I must admit that I was initially disappointed in being so categorized [as an extremist]. But as I continued to think about the matter, I gradually gained a bit of satisfaction from being considered an extremist... Was not Abraham Lincoln an extremist: "This nation cannot survive half slave and half free." Was not Thomas Jefferson an extremist: "We hold these truths to be self-evident, that all men are created equal." So the question is not whether we will be extremists but what kind of extremist will we be. Will we be extremists for the preservation of injustice — or will we be extremists for the cause of justice?

For we must come to see that peace is not merely the absence of some negative force, it is the presence of a positive force. True peace is not merely the absence of tension, but it is the presence of justice and brotherhood.

{ "Love, Law, and Civil Disobedience" — extract from an address before the annual meeting of the Fellowship of the Concerned, November

1961 }

But we simply cannot have peace

in the world without mutual respect.

Here is the true meaning and value of compassion and nonviolence when it helps us to see the enemy's point of view, to hear his questions, to know his assessment of ourselves. For from his view we may indeed see the basic weaknesses of our own condition, and if we are mature, we may learn and grow and profit from the wisdom of the brothers who are called the opposition.

{ A "Time to Break Silence" — extract from the historic address delivered at the Riverside Church in New York City exactly a year before King was assassinated, April

1967 }

Life and history give eloquent testimony to the fact that conflicts are never resolved without trustful give and take on both sides.

We can no longer afford to worship the god of hate or bow before the altar of retaliation.

Somehow we must be able to stand up before our most bitter opponents and say: "We shall match your capacity to inflict suffering by our capacity to endure suffering. We will meet your physical force with soul force. Do to us what you will and we will still love you… But be assured that we'll wear you down by our capacity to suffer, and one day we will win our freedom. We will not only win freedom for ourselves; we will so appeal to your heart and conscience that we will win you in the process, and our victory will be a double victory."

{ Extract from a "Christmas Sermon on Peace," December

1967 }

If I hit you and you hit me, and I hit you back and you hit me back, and go on, you see, that goes on ad infinitum. It just never ends. Somewhere somebody must have a little sense, and that's the strong person. The strong person is the person who can cut off the chain of hate, the chain of evil.

To believe in nonviolence does not mean that violence will not be inflicted upon you. The believer in nonviolence is the person who will willingly allow himself to be the victim of violence, but he will never inflict it upon another. He lives by the conviction that through his suffering and cross bearing, the social situation may be redeemed.

{ "Advice for Living" column — extract from King's last column for *Ebony* magazine after doctors advised him to limit his commitments following his stabbing, October

1958 }

People are often surprised to learn that I am an optimist. They know how often I have been jailed, how frequently the days and nights have been filled with frustration and sorrow, how bitter and dangerous are my adversaries. They expect these experiences to harden me into a grim and desperate man. They fail, however, to perceive the sense of affirmation generated by the challenge of embracing struggle and surmounting obstacles.

{ Extract from "A Testament of Hope" essay — published posthumously

1968}

There is nothing wrong with power if power is used correctly… And one of the great problems of history is that the concepts of love and power have usually been contrasted as opposites — polar opposites — so that love is identified with a resignation of power, and power with a denial of love.

Now power properly understood is nothing but the ability to achieve purpose. It is the strength required to bring about social, political, and economic change.

What is needed is a realization that power without love is reckless and abusive, and love without power is sentimental and anemic. Power at its best is love implementing the demands of justice, and justice at its best is power correcting everything that stands against love.

{ "Where Do We Go from Here?" — extract from King's last Southern Christian Leadership Conference (SCLC) presidential address before his death }

True altruism is more than the capacity to pity; it is the capacity to sympathize. Pity may represent little more than the impersonal concern which prompts the mailing of a check, but true sympathy is the personal concern which demands the giving of one's soul.

If you want to be important — wonderful. If you want to be recognized — wonderful. If you want to be great — wonderful… You only need a heart full of grace. A soul generated by love.

We must develop and maintain the capacity to forgive. He who is devoid of the power to forgive is devoid of the power to love.

It's not merely an emotional something.
Love is creative, understanding goodwill
for all men. It is the refusal to defeat
any individual.

{ "Loving Your Enemies" — extract from a sermon
delivered at Dexter Avenue Baptist Church, Montgomery,
Alabama, November

1957}

Love is the only force capable of

transforming an enemy into a friend.

Hatred and bitterness can never cure the disease of fear; only love can do that. Hatred paralyzes life; love releases it. Hatred confuses life; love harmonizes it. Hatred darkens life; love illumines it.

Man has the capacity to do right as well as wrong, and his history is path upward, not downward.

Courage faces fear and thereby masters it. Cowardice represses fear and is thereby mastered by it. Courageous men never lose the zest for living even though their life situation is zestless; cowardly men, overwhelmed by the uncertainties of life, lose the will to live.

{ "Antidotes for Fear" — extract from a sermon
delivered at the time of the Montgomery bus protests }

There is a maxim in the law — justice too long delayed is justice denied.

{ Extract from "If the Negro Wins, Labor Wins" —
address in Bal Harbour, Florida, December

1961 }

Every man lives in two realms, the internal and the external. The internal is that realm of spiritual ends expressed in art, literature, morals, and religion. The external is that complex of devices, techniques, mechanisms, and instrumentalities by means of which we live. Our problem today is that we have allowed the internal to become lost in the external. We have allowed the means by which we live to outdistance the ends for which we live.

We must rapidly begin the shift from a "thing-orientated" society to a "person-orientated" society. When machines and computers, profit motives and property rights are considered more important than people, the giant triplets of racism, materialism, and militarism are incapable of being conquered.

If we assume that life is worth living, if we assume that mankind has a right to survive, then we must find an alternative to war.

No individual can live alone; no nation can live alone, and as long as we try, the more we are going to have war in this world.

One does not need to be a profound scholar to be open-minded, nor a keen academician to engage in an assiduous pursuit for truth.

The potential beauty of human life is constantly made ugly by man's ever-recurring song of retaliation.

Wisdom born of experience should tell us that war is obsolete.

It is no longer a choice between violence and nonviolence in this world; it's nonviolence or nonexistence.

{ "I See the Promised Land" sermon (also referred to as "I've Been to the Mountaintop") — extract from King's last sermon, delivered on the eve of his assassination, in Memphis, Tennessee, April 3,

1968 }

94

CHARITY

A royalty from the sale of this book will be shared between the Tygerberg Children's Hospital and Philani Clinic on behalf of Archbishop Desmond Tutu, and the Estate of Martin Luther King, Jr.

ACKNOWLEDGMENTS

The publisher is grateful for permissions to reproduce material subject to copyright. Every effort has been made to trace the copyright holders and the publisher apologizes for any unintentional omission. We would be pleased to hear from any not acknowledged here and undertake to make all reasonable efforts to include the appropriate acknowledgment in any subsequent editions.

Words of Dr. King copyright © Dr. Martin Luther King, Jr., all copyrights renewed Coretta Scott King and the heirs to the Estate of Dr. Martin Luther King, Jr. Used by permission of the heirs to the Estate of Dr. Martin Luther King, Jr. and Writers House, LLC, New York City. Extract from Nobel Prize speech copyright © The Nobel Foundation 1964. Images of Dr. King used by permission of the heirs to the Estate of Dr. Martin Luther King, Jr. and the following copyright holders: p. 6 © Getty Images; pp. 8, 13, 16, 19, 30 (also cover), 38–39, 41, 47, 54, 59, 73 and 80 © Time Life Pictures/Getty Images; pp. 21 and 67 © Bettmann/CORBIS;pp. 88–89 © Flip Schulke/CORBIS. Image of Desmond Tutu (p. 2) © Matt Hoyle.

Archbishop Tutu for his generous support of the Ubuntu Collection; and Lynn Franklin, Archbishop Tutu's literary agent, for her kind assistance with the series.

The King Center, and in particular Leslie Chavous, Licensing Coordinator. Established in 1968 by Coretta Scott King, The King Center is the official living memorial dedicated to the advancement of the legacy of Dr. Martin Luther King, Jr., leader of America's greatest nonviolent movement for justice, equality and peace. More than 650,000 visitors from all over the world are drawn annually to the King Center to pay homage to Dr. King, view unique exhibits illustrating his life and teachings and visit the King Center's Library, Archives, his final resting place, his birth home, gift shop and other facilities. Located in Atlanta's Martin Luther King, Jr. National Historic Site, the King Center utilizes diverse communications media, including books, audio and video cassettes, film, television, CDs and web pages, to reach out far beyond its physical boundaries to educate people all over the world about Dr. King's life, work, and his philosophy and methods of nonviolent conflict-reconciliation and social change. www.thekingcenter.org

Mike Nicol for his insightful biographical essay. Mike Nicol has had a distinguished career both in South Africa and in the UK as an author, journalist and poet. He is the author of four critically acclaimed novels published in South Africa, the US, the UK, France and Germany. His best-known nonfiction work is his book on *Drum* magazine, *A Good-Looking Corpse* (Secker & Warburg, 1991), widely regarded as one of the most compelling accounts of the vibrant culture in the black townships of the 1950s.

Thanks also to Jenny Clements for text research and Simon Elder for picture research.

SELECT BIBLIOGRAPHY

Baker, Patricia, *Martin Luther King* (Wayland Publishers, London, 1974).
Carson, Clayborne (ed.), *Papers of Martin Luther King, Jr., Vol. II* (University of California Press, Berkeley, 1992).
— *The Autobiography of Martin Luther King, Jr.* (Little, Brown and Company, London, 1999).
— and Holloran, Peter (eds.), *A Knock at Midnight — Inspiration from the Great Sermons of Martin Luther King, Jr.* (Abacus, London, 2000).
Fairclough, Adam, *Martin Luther King* (Cardinal, London, 1990).
Garrow, David J., *Bearing the Cross — Martin Luther King, Jr. and the Southern Christian Leadership Conference* (Jonathan Cape, London, 1988).
King, Martin Luther, Jr., *Strength to Love* (Harper & Row, New York, 1963).
— and Washington J. M. (ed.), *A Testament of Hope — The Essential Writings and Speeches of Martin Luther King, Jr.* (Harper & Row, San Francisco, 1986).
— and Coretta Scott King (ed.), *In My Own Words* (Hodder & Stoughton, London, 2002).

NOTES FOR THE BIBLIOGRAPHIC ESSAY

1 Carson, Clayborne, ed., *The Autobiography of Martin Luther King, Jr.*, 226; 2 Garrow, David J., *Bearing the Cross*, 577; 3 Ibid. 35; 4 Carson, Clayborne, ed., *The Autobiography of Martin Luther King, Jr.*, 60 ; 5 Ibid. 77/78; 6 Ibid. 80; 7 Baker, Patricia, *Martin Luther King*, 46; 8 Garrow, David J., *Bearing the Cross*, 553 ; 9 Ibid. 515; 10 Ibid. 621; 11 Carson, Clayborne, (ed.), *The Autobiography of Martin Luther King, Jr.*, 226.